HORSE MUSIC

MATTHEW SWEENEY

Horse Music

BLOODAXE BOOKS

ISBN: 978 1 85224 967 0

First published 2013 by
Bloodaxe Books Ltd,
Highgreen,
Tarset,
Northumberland NE48 1RP.

www.bloodaxebooks.com
For further information about Bloodaxe titles
please visit our website or write to
the above address for a catalogue.

Supported by
**ARTS COUNCIL
ENGLAND**

Cover design: Neil Astley & Pamela Robertson-Pearce.

Printed in Great Britain by
Bell & Bain Limited, Glasgow, Scotland.

for Mary

ACKNOWLEDGEMENTS

Acknowledgements are due to the editors of the following publications where some of these poems first appeared: *Alhambra Poetry Calendar*, *The Best British Poetry 2011* (Salt Publishing, 2011), *BigCityLit*, *Blackbox Manifold*, *The Bow Wow Shop*, *Cork Literary Review*, *The Dark Horse*, *The Echo Room*, *Free Verse*, *The Guardian*, *Guernica*, *The Irish Times*, *London Magazine*, *London Review of Books*, *Magma*, *The New Yorker*, *The North*, *The Poetry Archive*, *Poetry Ireland Review*, *Poetry London*, *Poetry Review*, *Poetry Wales*, *Prairie Schooner*, *The Rialto*, *The Shop*, *Southword*, *The Spectator*, *The Stinging Fly*, *The Ulster Tatler*, *Upstairs at Duroc*, *The Warwick Review*, *Wasafiri*. and *The Wolf*.

'A History of Glassblowing' was awarded joint second prize in the 2010 National Poetry Competition.

'Fans' appeared in the bilingual selection, *Rosa Milch*, published by Berlin Verlag in 2008.

CONTENTS

There was an old man of Whitehaven,
Who danced a quadrille with a Raven;
But they said – 'It's absurd, to encourage this bird!'
So they smashed that Old Man of Whitehaven.

EDWARD LEAR

Naked, exposed to the frost of this most unhappy of ages,
with an earthly vehicle, unearthly horses, old man that I
am, I wander astray.

FRANZ KAFKA, 'A Country Doctor'
(tr. Edwin & Willa Muir)

Whssht, and away, and over the green
Scampered a shape that never was seen

WALTER DE LA MARE

The Emperor's Dwarves

The chimes of midnight fade from the Clocktower.
The Emperor's drunken dwarves are not abed.
Someone should take the schnapps off them,
open the window, fling it down Schloßberg
to smash against a yellow-flowering tree.
They are dancing, they are singing, fighting.
The Easter ham is piled high on a plate,
and, mouth full, one dwarf does handstands
while their Pekinese jumps and barks.
Someone should call in the Imperial Guard
to grab each dwarf and bring to the dungeon –
a good place for hangovers in puny men.
Where are their flutes, their mandolins, violins?
Why is Mendel not writing those ballads
that the Emperor's wife values so much?
Rico, the Head Dwarf, is asleep on the floor,
an empty bottle overturned beside him.
This is no way to celebrate holy Easter.
The painted eggs are flying through the air.
The Pekinese howls as the clock chimes one.

The Vintner's Boat

The vintner rowed his boat
as close to the lake's shore
as he dared, and in the prow
stood a five-litre bottle
of his Cabernet Franc *Barrique.*
A big man, he powered on,
past sunbathers, past sleepers,
past fisherfolk, whose lines
he took care to avoid.
Behind him, a school of perch
grew in numbers, as if all
were reincarnated drinkers.
The odd shout encouraged him
to launch paper aeroplanes
carrying his email address.
One man swam after him
but was poked by an oar
and called a wine pirate.
The vintner whistled a *chanson,*
between swigs from a hipflask –
his prizewinning *Lie.*
Overhead, the egg-sun fried.
He took a bite from a *saucisson*
and rowed his red boat on.

The Village of Scarecrows

In the village of scarecrows
every house has one
and some belong to no house,
stand there meeting the cars
that sometimes slow down.
And no scarecrow looks like another,
some are tall, some small,
one presents a smiling visage,
another a scowl, one is the priest,
another is the policeman,
a third is the village madman
and guards the vintner's cave,
then graces the label
of his best wine, which
the creator of the scarecrows
drinks free every night
to inspire him to new forms
of scarecrow, which he tests
on his two pet crows,
then plants before dawn.

Confiscated
(for Chris Rice)

Because the Count shot the President
the Chateau was confiscated.
All the art went to the Museum.
The Estate and grounds were sold off
to a business consortium in France,
everything except the vineyards.

You'll have read about those vineyards.
They were coveted by the President,
and by every vintner in France.
It's astonishing they weren't confiscated,
or the Count wasn't forced to sell off.
They're written up in the Museum.

It's really not a bad little Museum,
right in the middle of the vineyards.
There's a brochure about it in every cell of
the local prison, which the President
opened before the Chateau was confiscated,
and before his body went to France.

He wanted to be buried in France –
his will is displayed in the Museum
next to shots of the Chateau being confiscated
juxtaposed with shots of the vineyards,
and looming over all, a bust of the President
which the Curator wanted sold off.

In fact, he wanted the whole lot sold off.
He'd found a buyer in France,
a woman who said she'd loved the President
and whose riches would save the Museum.
She also wanted to buy the vineyards,
and the Chateau that was confiscated.

The Count denied that it was confiscated.
He believed it had been sold off
and the money buried in the vineyards.
He ranted this in his prison in France.
He wrote letters to the Museum,
saying he hadn't shot the President.

The President's dead, the Chateau's confiscated,
the Museum wants everything sold off,
and all France knows I've got the vineyards!

Ghost

A man egged another on to kill him,
then appeared as a vengeful ghost,
whispering to his killer that the cost
of his enjoyment of that final whim
would be nothing less than suicide.
No lifetime spent in prison's care,
not even a blast of the electric chair
would do. He'd need to have died
by the same hand as the other man,
on the same day, in the same place,
and if the killer should prefer to run,
the ghost would float before his face,
hissing that he was no one, no one,
and he would never win this race.

The Photos on the Wall

The photos on the wall all tell
the same story – how a horse
galloped past the lighthouse into the sea.
It was an ex-racehorse, tired of stud –
name *Fancydancer*, three times winner
of the Irish National, with different jockeys,
all surnamed Crowe. Those in the know
say that horse would have won riderless –
say it was lamed in the night by a rival stable
to stop it winning everything in England.
I say the photos on the wall tell it all –
those races were practice for this final gallop,
this last captured splash into the sea.
How the photographer knew to be there,
how he had a boat ready to follow
the now-swimming horse, is beyond me,
but the photos show each stage – the head
held high out of the water, the hoof-frothed foam,
the long creature tiring, mouth-opening, sinking,
and finally the buoy, last photo on the wall.

The Tunnel

(for Seamus Heaney)

Into the tunnel he went,
led by a torch, a tiny
silver torch bought in Crete.

In his pocket was a scalpel
and a folded bag. His mobile
was slotted into his belt.

Earphones brought him Coltrane's
gnarled tones. He wriggled
past a dog's skull, a tennis ball,

a dusty copy of the bible.
An edition of *North* was propped
against the wall. He checked,

it was signed. He slithered on,
his beam now bouncing off mosaic
mirrors on the low ceiling.

As the sax swirled, he hummed
along, sniffing the trapped air,
feeling ahead, as if the light

would miss something vital,
would blank out a sign.
He stuck gum in his mouth.

Chewing, he muscled on, past
a framed photo of bombed Berlin,
a warped tennis racquet, a gun.

A map of Europe appeared on the wall,
then disappeared. A voice rode over
Coltrane, counting to a hundred,

and at the hundred, he emerged
into a red chamber. He stood up
and walked to the seated corpse.

The Poison Dwarfs

The poison dwarfs are in the room.
The poison dwarfs are in the room.
They crowd round me. They stand there
without moving, yet get ever closer.
They are clones, with the same face.
They say nothing, simply stare –
big black eyes beneath plucked brows,
just-parted lips that will not smile,
that certainly will not be kissed.
That face is familiar from somewhere.
Who has taken their arms, their hands,
and why are their legs so stuntedly short?
They make me see pink spots flickering
on their pale green suits, their faces.
The poison dwarfs are in the room,
getting closer, though they never move.
Their shadows are their reinforcements.
Their stare is mutating into a scream.

The Warning

That sizzling morning, I lay on the lawn,
beneath the totem pole I'd brought back
from Nevada, and painted white and black,
to ward off ghouls, ghosts, and evil men.

I had Coltrane playing from the hallway
and was humming along. The black cat
was poking and hissing at the white cat,
when a crow landed a couple of feet away.

Both cats scarpered when he opened his beak
and cawed, dropping a piece of red paper,
to be exact, a neatly folded page of notepaper,
as I saw when I stretched out an arm to check

what he'd brought. It was typed in blue ink,
and purported to be a warning in rhyme –
including archipelagos of identical rhyme –
that this garden and others would soon stink

of putrefaction, and I and the cats would lie,
decomposing, beneath the striped pole,
the ludicrously inappropriate, exotic pole
that was supposed to enable me not to die,

at least for a century. That's what the man
said when I'd bought it, the Native American
who claimed he was the only real American,
he and his dwindling kind. I needed that man

now. He was one who could talk to crows,
I was sure. Hadn't he shouted at an eagle,
a symbolic, black and white, bald eagle,
that *was* America. I loved his long nose,

his lopsided dance under the full moon,
tipsy with whiskey, then his croaked song,
his sharing of that famous, patriotic song
I forgot as soon as we stood under the sun.

Anyway, the crow flapped and flew away,
without a sound. The cats scuttled back,
lovey-dovey now. I stretched my long back
and got to my feet, to make my sad way

out from under the totem pole. Why me?,
I asked, as I walked back to the cool house,
the suddenly transformed forever house.
There was no answer from the boiling sky.

The cats ran in, black and white, around me.
I looked out at the black and white pole,
the beautiful, appropriate, necessary pole.
I poured myself an unseemly early whiskey.

A Song about a Crow

The boy watched the crow peck at the ground,
tugging out a worm which it swallowed,
then digging around, hunting for some more
He saw the grey feathers on the neck and back,
the same grey as the seat of his patched pants,
while the black patch on his right knee
matched the black of the crow's main feathers.
The boy's bare feet looked at the crow's claws.
Should he go over and help it find worms?
Should he run and take it up in his hands,
then bring it back to the red houseboat
to keep there, tied on a string, as his pet,
feeding it worms, speaking Finnish to it,
teaching it to trust him and fly ahead,
always returning to him standing on deck,
while his bearded father negotiated the locks
waiting for the water level to rise or fall,
barely looking as the crow landed on the boy's
shoulder, with a caw that earned it a stroke
and a song that he'd made up about a crow?

The Alchemist

(for Elmar Schenkel)

High over the Atlantic I remember
being brought to visit the alchemist –
a thin man with a crow-beak nose
who'd gone to Oxford with my grandpa,
then had made his name curing sick bees.
I can see again his pink cottage
down on the rocks, beyond Padstow,
with the black goat grazing outside.

I can hear his high-pitched laugh
as he goes off, whisky-glass in hand,
to bring back a drawer full of gold,
shining blobs of all sizes, which he
spread out on the glass coffee-table.
Here, he said, handing me the biggest,
Buy yourself a midget submarine –
there's more where that came from.

I pocketed the smooth nugget, wishing
I could stay and become his apprentice,
but my grandpa hugged the alchemist
and brought me to the railway station.
As for my gold, I didn't get to enjoy it –
my mother used it up on the new kitchen.
I flick on the flight-attendant light,
then ask the hostess for a large whisky.

A History of Glassblowing

The records show that in Shanghai
at the end of the Yuan Dynasty,
the year 1364, a glassblower blew
a mermaid that came to life, and swam
away. And in Cologne, in 1531, a team
of glassblowers blew an orchestra,
instruments and all, and these played.
Then on Hokkaido, in 1846, a blind
monk blew his own Buddha to pray to,
and the next day he was able to see.
In Natchez, in 1901, a glassblower
blew a paddleboat with gamblers in it,
one of them lying dead. And in Oaxaca,
in 1929, a small version of the Sierra
Madre was blown, with golddiggers
on its lower slopes, and the whole
town filled with gold. In Letterkenny,
in 1965, a woman blew a flock
of glass sheep, wool and all, each
of them with a tinkly baa. In 1993,
in Séte, the harbour glassblower
blew a lighthouse with its own light,
and in 2004, in Timişoara, three
glassies blew a new solar system
that they let float up and away.

The Blue Hammock

Behind the toolshed, among the nettles,
and rusting horseshoes, I buried the key.

The white dog watched me, whimpering,
as if he disapproved of what I was doing

but when I unearthed a bone and threw it
he bounded away, barking, into the field.

I replaced the spade in the shed, strode off
to the blue hammock, and climbed into it.

Swaying from side to side, I began to hum
the tune from the first spaghetti Western,

where Clint raises his poncho and shoots,
then lights up another cigarillo. Above me

the silver birch with my initials stretched
upward to its far-off father, the moon.

They would never, ever find that key, and
in the morning I would head for Lisbon,

where I'd rent a room in hilly Alfama,
then translate the entire work of Brecht.

The seagulls are huge there, and musical.
The crows spend most time on the ground.

Fish and Chips

(for Tim Turnbull)

My friend used to have fish and chips
five times a week, so he'd know
the good stuff, and sure enough, he took me
past the Isle of Ola to a yachty harbour
called Anstruther, with a poky, photogenic
lighthouse, and a team of synchronised
swimming dogs, and a fish and chip shop
given the blue ribbon of Scotland –
oh, the haddock deep-fried in batter
lighter than a moth-wing, a wafer,
and the *ack* of that gull on the lamppost
as we circumambulated the boats,
fantasising about stealing the finest one,
sailing it to the Shetlands, and staying there,
founding a radio station, broadcasting
bird poetry, including paeans to the haddock,
the hake, the halibut, the cod, the lowly
mackerel, even, all the while perfecting
the deep-frying of each of these fish
with chunks of local, island potatoes –
till the ferry draws in from Aberdeen,
and the official tasters step ashore.

Horse Music

Hearing of horses speaking Irish on the island
he took a boat out there, paid an islander
daft money to lead him to the westernmost field
where a shy pair of russet ponies stood head-
to head on a hilly mound that jutted out over
the leaping froth of the Atlantic. He pretended
not to notice them, said goodbye to his guide
in Irish picked up from books in southern Spain –
his lifetime's hobby – then sat on his hunkers,
listening hard, but either the horses were quiet
or he needed to get closer. He waited until a
gang of screaking gulls got the horses neighing,
then over he went, soothing them with murmurs,
stroking them, until one said in fluent Irish
to the other 'This hairy fellow could be OK,
but we can't trust him, can't trust any of them.
Two legs? I mean, imagine yourself like that.'
The other whinnied, and hoofed the ground,
then began to sing a song, a wrenching lament
for a red-haired woman, that intensified
when the second horse joined in, so the man
slipped away, head down, back to the harbour.

Communiqué

(for little Nell)

Tiny-eared, tiny-fingered one,
the moon is there for you to visit,
the hotels at the bottom of the sea.

You will learn to savour Antrim wine
while eating deep-fried, nettle-wrapped
jellyfish on baked dock leaves.

Ah, the music that you'll listen to,
while levitating in the garden, the art
you'll see floating in the sky.

Ambassadors from other planets
will grace your phone TV screen,
with no translation needed. No,

language barriers will be blasted,
the dog will confess to you
that he bit the travelling chef.

The email chip in your brain
will receive messages from the dead,
and will even answer them.

So this is a first communiqué,
one sent early. Take your time,
tiny one, but do respond to me.

Haiku for My Father

1

I telephone home –
the voice on the ansaphone
is his from the tomb.

2

I ask did he hear
those last words I whispered to
his comatose ear.

3

That cut on his hand
as he entered the long box –
is it on the mend?

4

Who's cutting his hair
down there in the freezing dark
without any air?

5

His nails also grow –
what about the blackened one
on his little toe?

6

That bottle of wine
I served with the Xmas goose –
I'll bring it again.

7

I will roast some lamb
and let it get way overdone –
to satisfy him.

8

If I try Irish
will he speak to me and say
I've granted his wish?

9

I want him to read
these lines I've written for him,
if he's really dead.

10

I call his number
that's saved on my mobile phone –
there is no answer.

In the Garden

(i.m my father)

While I was shawling the strawberries
with fine green netting, you told me
about the cow that swam to the island
to stand there mooing until the seals
came in close to add their own belling,
with the seagulls circling above, kao-
kaoing – and after you'd stared enough
you ran to the farmer, who didn't believe
until he saw for himself, then asked
if you'd row him out there, to ferry
the creature home, and you wouldn't,
saying it was too heavy, would sink
the boat, or at least would kick out,
sending all three of you overboard –
no, the Narin lifeboat had to be called
to bring the cow back to a cheering crowd.
I stood there visualising the whole film
as you spaded the bright new potatoes.

The Glass Chess Set

He woke to find a glass chess set
by his head, on the bedside table.
The vitamins had been removed,
the lamp shifted to the floor,
the two glasses of water were gone –
all this done without a noise.
He sat up to see it better.
Everything was glass – the board,
the pieces, half of these clear,
half opaque, as were the alternating
squares. He got out of bed to
stand above it. One opaque pawn
had advanced, the clear team
nearest to him had made no move.
It was his turn. Who was
his invisible opponent? He opened
the shutters to let light in,
recalling his last game of chess
with his father. It had been Xmas.
He'd lost, of course, as always.
Well, he remembered winning once,
then refusing to play for years.
He glimpsed the set's reflection
in the mirror, saw for a second
a shadow stood there, then it was gone.
He sat down, studied the board,
and slowly, moved a clear pawn.

Lunch in Alfama

(i.m. my mother)

Down the hill from Castelo de São Jorge
where the African King kept two lions
in a wing of the palace, and traps
were set for insolent, infidel besiegers,
we sat at a table on a restaurant terrace
and ordered grilled cuttlefish and sardines,
with a bottle of Dao white. A guitarist was
playing the zither tune from *The Third Man*
when I saw my mother advancing towards us.
What on earth was she doing in Lisbon?
Her hair was orange, she wore big blue
glasses and thick, carmine lipstick. I
moved a chair for her to sit and join us
but she scuttled past, ignoring me,
her eldest son. I stood and stared after her,
as a gang of pigeons swooped around me
like Hitchcock's stars, and the waiter
arrived with food I no longer wanted,
so I sank down and pushed it away,
gulping back a whole glass of the wine.

Sunday Morning

The Sunday morning bells
are clanging and clanking,
droning and echoing,
and somewhere a dog, a black
cocker spaniel is howling,
and my rotund grandmother
wants me to go to the shop,
before the crowd leaves Mass,
to buy her Woodbines and
Silvermints, and get myself
a Peggy's Leg, so as soon as
the bells die away, Bonzo
and I head up the road,
where his enemy, the goose
is waiting to charge out,
lunging at him, while I
kick at the jabbing neb
and shout, calling the dog
after me, as the farmer
stands in his door and laughs
till we cross to the other side
where the shop should be
but isn't, and the dog
has vanished, and the cash
in my hand is a different
currency, and hundreds of
houses, streets, squares are
all around me, so I run back
down, but the sea is gone,
then the bells start up again.

Snow, Ice

In spite of the snow, he powered his bike
down the freezing road, avoiding the dogs
that gambolled there, shitting and pissing,
barking and growling. He cursed them all,
their scarfed and gloved owners, too,
also the cars that passed him by too close,
the monster buses that wanted to crush him,
the fat cold moon in the smoggy sky above.

His mouth recalled the taste of brandy-balls,
sucked hard, rolled around, then splintered.
He saw his own dog, a black cocker, running
after his red child's bike; and the snow vulture
he created at the gate, then brought inside
to scare his granny who was trying to die
all those years ago, before he crossed the sea,
then another sea, then criss-crossed over

and back, to where he was cycling now
trying to get to a big frozen lake, where
a man dressed in black was skating round
and round and round, gouging a circle
through which he wanted to fall, to freeze
in the water and never come back out, no,
never, and so he pedalled harder, hoping
the ice was thick enough to wait for him.

Revenant

(for Ann Diver)

She came to her daughter in a dream,
asking to be dug up from her grave
and ferried to her cousin – who'd died
although she didn't seem to know this,
nor that her cousin's husband was gone.
No, she wanted to be brought to them,
and when a traffic-jam thwarted her,
she authorised a plan B – take her, she
said, to where they'd wanted to retire to
(although they'd never managed this),
And when this didn't work out either,
more traffic shit, roadworks, who knows...
she demanded to go back to her grave,
and be re-interred by her daughter.

The Bomb

They blew up my grave last night,
my bones went everywhere,
my startled spirit zipped through the sky
like a panicked crow in a storm.
What was the point of that? he cried
to the trees, and the unblasted stones
that stood upright, with names and dates,
while mine was in smithereens.

The cameras came to record the mess,
and included my ancient photos.
In all reports that went to the papers
they chose my least favourite ones,
but my spirit was annoyed at me,
saying it didn't matter. *There was no
shot of you in the grave*, he rasped,
and wasn't that the relevant one?

I wasn't sure of this but I was dead,
and he was hanging around. And he
was all that was left of me, although
now I had my doubts. But how these
had manifested themselves
was a mystery – unless it was the bomb
that had shook me back together again
in the maddest way? Then, what was I?

The Rising

The totem pole towered above the birches
whose silver bark was marked by the moon,
and the dead fox lying on the highway
saw the face on the pole begin to smile
and keep on smiling, till the creature rose
to run and disappear deep into the forest.

The Suckling Pig

The suckling pig came flying over the wall
of the beleaguered city. It was still warm.
The smell drew a crowd of armed men
followed by crying women. The boys
roasting fat rats on spits let them burn.
A hand reached for a leg of the piglet
but was sliced off with a longsword.
Shouting rose in pitch to a hullabaloo
which was stabbed into stillness by a voice
saying 'Only the Governor gets to eat it,
him and his wife, and maybe the Reverend.'

The Governor stood there in his wide hat.
He poked the pig with a finger, licked this
and looked at his wife, while the Reverend
blessed what they were going to consume.
'What if it's poisoned?' said a boy,
who was shushed. A soldier took a dagger
from his belt, wiped it on his tunic,
cut off a juicy chunk and devoured it.
He grinned at the Governor who beckoned
the man to carve all and distribute it
to the three while the citizens looked on.

Sausages

There are six of you, inhabiting the same gut,
twisted separate. You lie on the white plate,
coiled, like fat, sleeping worms, waiting

waiting on the hot pan with spitting oil
after the knife frees you. In each of you
is my long-dead grandfather, and the pigs

the pigs he killed, then cleavered in the yard,
their last squeals too, then the hard journey,
twice, through the mincer to the big bowl

the big bowl where chopped onion joins them,
also wild thyme, garlic, breadcrumbs, parsley,
salt, and a good dash of pepper. The pig gut

the pig gut is removed and cleaned in water,
so the mixture can be squeezed in, the gut
twisted at intervals, and you are ready

ready, so my grandfather lights a cigarette,
opens a bottle of Guinness and swigs it,
sitting down at the far end of the table

the table I will sit at when you're browned,
and I'll eat you, one by one, with mustard,
raising a black glass to my grandfather.

Pan on the Pink Bridge

I saw Pan today on the pink bridge
waving his red boots. I heard him
before I saw him, tootling his flute,
up there, over the dual carriageway,
with its cars beetling to Fermoy,
to Portlaoise, to Dublin. It was a Chinese
jig he was playing, and my feet,
like his hidden hooves, were dancing
so much I had to stop driving, then
get out to prance on the hard shoulder,
alongside the others bouncing there,
howling out in tune to the notes of Pan,
who slowly began to be swallowed by fog,
through which his muffled music continued,
less Chinese now, more Steppes-Russian,
until with a final flourish it stopped.
After some minutes, we rejoined our cars,
drove away, peering through the murk,
glancing in our mirrors, listening hard,
grateful for this visit of Great God Pan.

Ballad of the Horse and Wine

A horse neighed a loud hello
    as I went by with wine.
He did it to let me know
    he wanted what was mine.

I ignored him, and walked on
    with my sad half-case.
His neighs followed me down
    to a dim, castly place.

I was holed up there, with others,
    a ragtaggle bunch
of daughters, fathers, mothers,
    all now eating lunch.

I carried my clinking stash in,
    and one fellow got up
to snatch a bottle of the wine.
    Another grabbed a cup.

He filled this to the very brim!
    Before the rest could start
I retreated to my room,
    to calm my beating heart.

Then I saw the horse's head
    through the window glass
and heard how he neighed
    and refused to pass.

So I hurried out to him
    to feed him some wine,
whacking him on the bum
    as he glugged it down.

I retrieved the other bottles
    and felt like Lord Byron,
as the horse and I tottered
    to the Château de Chillon.

We finished them all there,
    then both fell asleep
by Lake Geneva's waters,
    one thousand feet deep.

The White Peacock at Schloß Eggenberg

I am white as the moon I shriek at
because it's up there, unassailable.

I am not like my gaudy brothers –
all blue, green, with those eyes spread out

when they fan open their tails, trying
to get those dowdy females to mate with them.

I wouldn't have any of those, even if
they came begging, which they won't.

I like to lie on the wall, my tail stretched out
behind me. If a child approaches, I lunge,

then I screech so loudly the others go quiet,
before coming in behind me, in a chorus.

They know never to approach me now,
since I pecked their ringleader to death.

It took weeks for the bloodstains to fade.
I spend most of my time high in the Schloß

on a windowsill I've made my own.
The others complain of the noise I make

but I ignore them, and shriek my heart out.
I might as well be up there on the moon.

The Twit

(for Mary)

The three-toed comb tamed the tangle,
unleashing a smile that bounced off the mirror
into my eyes, inspiring me to warble
a quivery, high-pitched, very silly song
about a tightrope-walking, hairy twit
traversing a ravine in a dumped sea of rain –
he was naked, of course, and his bare feet
gripped that slippy rope like a gorilla's
while he howled German insults at the sky,
thinking ahead to the huge bowl of goulash
he'd devour, in the company of a Villanyi red –
Villanyi, oh Villanyi, Hungary's finest
he twittered, as he advanced on his rope,
monitored by the vulture on the mountain.

Dr Quincy's Pleasure Emporium

Yes, I can see you, said the dwarf,
swinging from his chandelier,
flicking out his long orange hair,
as I lay under the leopard-skin sofa
entangled with a purple-eyed nymph.
A peacock uttered its long harsh cry
which ricocheted off the round mirror
encased in a copper ring, causing me
to curse and wriggle out, abandoning
the nymph who rolled up into a ball
and whimpered, as a white crow
flew round my head, then zipped off,
cawing me to follow into a yellow room
where a piper spun webs of green and blue,
and my nymph swirled with the dwarf
whose orange echoed the leaping flames
of the log-fire, in front of which
Dr Quincy swayed in a hammock, sipping
brandy, stroking the now quiet peacock
who suddenly laid an egg that was gold.

Other Worlds

My nose resembled a stinkhorn,
my teeth had more black than a piano's keys,
one eye was gone, my hair was electrocuted,
my voice, when I sang, made dogs howl,
so I deduced my future had to be in film.

I scanned *The Examiner* for an opening,
saw an invitation to inhabitants of other worlds.
Hitchhiking to the old port of Cobh,
fighting my way against a pipe band,
I presented myself at *The Titanic Arms*.

A bald man in a suit, with a red bow tie
but no shirt, scrutinised me at the door.
'You're uglier than a moose, you'll do.'
'I left my antlers at home,' I said
but he was hiccupping and his monkey farted.

I followed them up the stinky stairs.
Yuk, yuk, yuk shouted the speakers.
A parrot swooped down, shrieking my name.
Where were the cameras, the cameras?
A torrent of saltwater engulfed me.

How I Was Made 20 Years Younger

It had been years since I'd had a hard-on –
I blamed that witch I'd left my marriage for,
some spell she'd chanted, or the painful
eruption down there she'd gifted me,
or the kilometres I'd axed on the autobahn,
or the cases of Bordeaux I'd carried in –
whatever it was, the bedroom scared me,
too many women had entered it once,
but never twice, so I contacted Steinach –
I'd read about the success of his experiment;
I booked myself in for a vasectomy,
and two days later I'd a throbbing stonker –
couldn't wait to wield this implement.
All was well again in the house of hoopee,
so I decided I had to inform the unhappy –
I booked the Albert Hall, to give a lecture
How I Was Made 20 Years Younger.
I arrived in my blue suit, with a bow tie;
peeped from the wings to see the pews fill,
and right then it was decided I should die.

The Sleepwalker

The sleepwalker shot himself
on the bridge over the freeway,
while the cars sped on to Dallas.
A jogger who'd just passed
heard the shot, but kept running.
Hadn't he noticed the bulge
in the pyjamas pocket, the hard
set of the handsome face?
Back in the trailer-home, the dog
whined as if he saw the body
slump, and the blood seep out
into a pool that settled into a
red carpet, as the red sun hauled
itself, inch by inch, over the hilly
horizon, and a lone coyote howled.
A sleepy eagle hovered overhead,
replaying that dream of flying
into a volcano, down until his
wingtips were singed, and he
heard his shriek echo out, out
into the head of one asleep,
making him toss and turn, kick
the blankets off, leave the bed,
go into the night, grabbing the gun.

Nil

Saying nothing to no one, he climbed down
the bridge supports to the swollen River Lee.

A surly swan watched him, treading water.
Two ducks paddled quickly towards him.

He ignored them all, immersing himself in
the chilly flow, holding on to the stanchion

that rose above him to a drizzly heaven where
crows and gulls fought a squawky dogfight

and further up, a plane's white echo spelt out
a long, fuzzy nil. It was time to let go –

to kick away, splashing, letting the current
take him under the bridge which cars and walkers

crossed, each with somewhere to get to.
He laughed, swallowing a mucky mouthful.

It tasted of every wine he'd drunk, mixed
together, left uncorked for the years he'd lived.

To Ash Again

The urn turned upside down,
emptied out the ashes
and rolled away. The wind
grabbed each ash flake,
swooped it into the sky,
swirled it across the sea,
over fish, through gulls,
and on the other side
the ashes came together
to form the reborn man
who stole a bicycle,
pedalled up a mountain
and into a rushy tarn
where he drowned,
while the urn floated
across that same sea,
rolled across sand, fields,
then up that mountain, as trout
heaved the corpse out,
lightning bolts blasted it
to ash, which the urn ate,
then turned upside down...

Inside

(after Paul Klee's 'Wintertag, kurz vor Mittag')

It's my job to keep the smoke flowing
from our tower block – although I could
just catch the puffs of smoke that
float through the town, like baby clouds.
It's years since I've been outside in daylight,
but I see clearly the clock on the tower
stopped before noon, the Xmas trees
atop the hills and high-rises, the red
that's everywhere – the road, the roofs,
the occasional window, bits of the sky,
the sun. And I pine for each and every
lovely, outside bit of it.

The Key of Blue

(from a phrase of Dylan Thomas's)

He vanished into the Key of Blue –
a made man. Did he speak to you
before he ran, or did he disappear
without a word in anyone's ear?

What happened to his concubine
or his cellar of French wine?
Did his twin clear out his rooms
that he called *The Catacombs*?

Have you heard from him at all –
has he travelled as far as Nepal,
as he threatened to, one night
under a sick streetlight?

Or is he holed up in Scotland,
or on farmost Tory Island?
I want to pass on what I've seen
from inside the Key of Green.

Domestic

The gnomes are happy. They're banging
the pipes with their little hammers
as the heating comes on. Some days
they keep on banging, so I've no option
but switch the heating off, then find
that sheep-smelling jumper I bought
in Dingle when the snow swirled in.
Today they look like leaving their hammers
down. Is it they who've caused the sink
to leak water all over the kitchen floor.
And what about the grill that trips the power?
What next will they do? Crash my computer?
Turn the TV screen blank? Block the loo?
The smallest of bangs are coming now,
and sawing noises, metallic sighs,
pipey whistlings, tinny burps, hissings,
with lovely, leaden silences in between.
They're artists – I should record this.
Should invite people in, sit them down,
put tumblers of wine in their hands,
then go and switch the heating on.
But I know damn well what would happen –
nothing. They're like that, the gnomes.
They're not ones for publicity or acclaim.
Getting my attention is their only aim.

Sleeping

She's sleeping, and it's not late.
She was tired, very tired.
Those *fajitas*, preceded by
tequila, were far too much.
That film about dwarves
sent her to another place.
The bedclothes called her in.
The moon has a cloud ruff.

Beneath it, the rats scurry
round the overflown bin.
The phone rings, and I let it.
She did the dishes, then read
her China book, half-asleep.
Oh, oh, the poor houseplants –
I'd better water them, then
try to photograph the moon.

The Glass Eye

Not you, not him, but the other brother –
the one with the glass eye. Was he Fonsy?
Anyway, we'd laugh when he'd come down
from the hill to sell his hens at the mart.

He'd dance a jig to get the hens flapping.
He'd produce an egg from under his hat.
He'd sit a hen on his dog and hold it there,
cackling, as the mongrel danced and barked.

He'd ask us to watch the hens till he grabbed
a pint of the black stuff in the long-gone Glen
Hotel, and it wouldn't be one he'd stop at.
Soon he'd be belting out his only song –

where son Ted lost his leg to a big cannon-
ball, and we'd all join in on the chorus.
I never saw him sell a hen but he must have.
He always went home with less, even none.

Where is he now – Fonsy, or was it Benny?
I see him still, taking out the glass eye,
pretending to swallow it, or throw it deep
into the crowd, the socket gaping in his face.

The Sick Cow

The sick cow lay on the wet grass,
mooing and mooing, her belly
as big as the smallest moon of Saturn.
A black and white collie stood at the edge
of the sloped field, barking at her.
The cow paid as much attention as the sun
which did its best to spotlight the bloating.
Country music seeped from the hotel,
dancers twirling invisibly behind walls.
The sick cow began to roar, sending
the dog into a staccato volley of barks.
A walking couple stopped to stare,
then hurried up the road. The farmer
materialised in the field, then disappeared.
He returned in the passenger seat of a car,
whose driver removed from a bag a long
knife which he plunged in the cow's belly.
Gas and a foul smell whooshed out.
The cow mooed and roared, then lay
as still and quiet as a waiting roast.

The Lost Gold Medal

Munich Olympics 1972: there should have been
an Irish gold medal to go with Ronnie's
from Melbourne in 1956, my birth-year, give
or take four. The sport? Push-penny, or
push-halfpenny, as it had to be then, with a
2p banging a ½ p on a draughtsman's board,
the coins pinged by steel combs towards goals
marked in black pen. These decimal coins
were new in, and each wore a bird in a Celtic
knot design, stolen from the Book of Kells.
Zoom in to UCD in 1971, the testing ground.
Those old Georgian buildings on Earlsfort Tce.
The pride of the Engineering Faculty at battle
in private, till a university-wide championship
was flagged up all over the sprawling campus,
with entries coming in from Classics, English, Law,
you name it, all of them plonkers, using plastic
combs, credit cards, nailfiles, sawnoff rulers...
They entered like non-league clubs in the FA Cup
and unlike those, none of them prospered.

Cut to the semi-finals on a hot Friday in May,
not long after L'Escargot's second Gold Cup.
Three of the players were Engineering, one
Architecture, all men, the bulk of the fans women.
One match ended goalless, went to penalties,
the other ended 3:0, and that was me in the final
where I met my longhaired, moustachioed friend
who bet he'd beat me. Some chance! I scored early,
then sat back, *catenaccio*, warding off all attacks
till I scored again, with a viciously spinning
free-kick, after which my goalmouth had a wall.

Hoisted up, and carried, with cheers, to the pub
where a letter was drafted to the Irish Olympic
Committee, insisting it get push-penny added
to the Games so Ireland would win another gold.
As Google and History show, it didn't happen
but I'm still here, if in need of practice,
I have two mad, green shirts and green shoes,
draughtsman's boards must be cheap on eBay,
and I think the Mexicans still make steel combs.

The Naming of Horses

A grey horse lost a race today
by a neck. You want his name?
Ballylifen. And my home village
In North Donegal is Ballyliffin.
One of the names is misspelt –
is that why the grey horse lost?

As horse's names go, it's tame.
How about *Ravenclaw*, or
Trotting Weasel? They don't
win much either, but better
is *The Galloping Shoe*, or even
more so *Imsingingtheblues*.

I hear the Queen of England
names all her horses, and visits
them with bags of boiled sweets.
She's present at their genesis too.
She witnesses their begetting.
Her *Barbers Shop* was entered

in the Gold Cup, but lost out to
Kauto Star. And who named him?
Are there jobs for horse namers?
Can I get one? Here's a few of
my suggestions: *Fancydancer*,
Ricochet, *Madmanonthemoon*.

Burning

Walking up the hill in the rain
I smell burning – is it flesh?
I'm nearing the butchers. Has he
begun a spin-off kebab operation
and is still learning about coals?
But no, sniffing harder, this smell
is other – might it be human flesh?
Am I spontaneously combusting?
I thought I'd had a head-cold
but clearly, underneath, a volcano
has been erupting – one I've
anticipated all my life, ever since
those Dickens novels I borrowed,
one by one, as a child, from
my aunt's library. I begin to run,
closing the umbrella, to let
the rain at me, swatting my head,
my sides, the top of my back,
half-choking on the smoke that
clouds me. I reach the garden,
dive on the lawn to roll around
like a dog and howl like one
until I notice the smoke is gone,
I'm not hot, in fact I'm shivering,
and my breathing is normal.
I've been let off! Shamed, I slouch
to the front door, let myself in,
and go straight up to the shower.

Waiting

I seem to spend my whole life waiting –
waiting on money to come in, on mail to arrive,
on my partner to return from her date
with the lover I will soon find out about.
What's waiting but sitting in Purgatory
if not Limbo? I'd like to climb a lamppost
with a polar bear cub and hum sea shanties
till the Fire Brigade brings me down.
I'd like to knife my partner, the postman,
my publisher, the bank teller, my neighbour.
One day I'll emigrate to Antarctica
and befriend the penguins there. I'll write
a treatise on solitude and onanism,
on the pleasures of roaring at icebergs.
Right now I want to run through the streets
with an axe, grinning, but hacking no one.
I want to roll around in the melting snow.
Waiting? It's all the time on Death Row.
It's the thoughts of a tree in December.
Do you have any idea how ice forms,
or how a mind can shape and fire a bullet?

The Lake

Seeing no one about, no boat on the lake,
he braked. Locking the car, zipping his coat,
he walked down to the reeds at the water's edge.
He sat on his hunkers there, wanting his gloves,
scanning the lake's farther shore, the few houses,
the absolute lack of a jetty, a pier.
He thought of the lakes of Italy, of Switzerland –
how crowded the shores were, how many boats.
A long-legged heron glided in to land.
A dog behind him barked itself hoarse.
He saw the trees growing out of the water.
He picked his spot, seeing the house's shape,
the powder-blue jetty, the white speedboat.
He wondered how many trout were in there.
He wondered how many he'd have to bribe
to get the planning OK. He didn't care.
Without looking, he'd found what he wanted
and he would have it, that was sure.
He took his mobile out and photographed the site,
then briskly, smiling, he walked back to his car.

The Last Day of Summer

They hung the cat at dawn on the last day of summer.
They chorused out a dirge when it stopped kicking,
then all together flung their bottles out into the lake.
Miko held up a hand lacerated by the cat's claws,
as if it was a trophy. They snapped it with their mobiles,
allowing him alone to punch the swinging corpse.
'What now?' bellowed Heike. 'It's a baby of a day.
Tomorrow we disperse across this great big land.
Let's have a morning to light up the winter evenings.'
'We agree,' said the giant twins, 'Let's kill someone.'
A gust of laughter shook the dangling feline
as an elderly jogger in a red tracksuit hove into view.

On the Way to Potsdam

On the way to Potsdam I met a fox.
It was sitting in the corner of the S-Bahn carriage.
I looked around to see who its owner was —
every German has at least two dogs
so it made sense for someone to diversify.
No one was glancing at the fox, except me,
and it was me, only me, the fox was appraising.

Sure enough, when I got off at Potsdam
the fox immediately trotted after me.
I stopped, looked back, it stopped and stared.
Its eyes were brown pools of turf-water,
its face was a gypsy's who plays the guitar
so I walked on, knowing it would follow me,
and together we reached the Palace of Sanssouci.

The Fall

Screaming and roaring, the plane fell from the sky,
everyone on it knowing they would die,

and the gang of Turkish youths kicking a ball
on Sonnenallee didn't see it fall

till it broke up into bits on top of them
and they, who were not en route for Rome,

died with those who were, as a plague of sirens
arrived from everywhere at bleak Neukölln

while the grim *Polizei* roped off the street,
bits of whose houses lay in piles at their feet,

and the TV cameras congregated in force
with the commentators shouting themselves hoarse

to shocked ears and eyes all over the planet –
especially one man who was meant to be on it

but slept in, and flung his phone at the wall,
then kissed it for sussing the plane would fall

and called the woman he'd recently ended with,
begging her to meet him forthwith

at the Berlin Zoo, where they'd go and stand
by the panther's cage, and he'd ask for her hand.

Heckewald

Heckewald ist tod. Heckewald is dead,
no more to build on there. His compact flat
lies empty, the floor unbrushed, unwashed,
the sheets on the bed just as he left them,
the drained beer bottles piled up, waiting
to be brought back to redeem their *Pfand*,
and new, full bottles bought in their stead.
No, Heckewald is done with beer-drinking.
Heckewald is finished watching Germany
fight its way at the World Cup Finals,
with the flag-waving cars blowing horns
all the way down Hauptstrasse, and girls
in hotpants dancing outside the pubs.
Heckewald will eat no more *Currywurst*,
as he rushes to the U-Bahn in the morning.
He will sit no longer in front of the screen
in the internet café, throwing up picture
after picture of women he might meet.
He will not shout again at bus-drivers
who take off as he reaches his stop.
Where has he vanished to, Heckewald?
Has someone knifed him in Neukölln
as he waited on the night-bus home,
or has he been caught up in a bombing?
He always had a finger in the uprising,
that never happened. He wanted so much.
What am I to do with the mail that's come,
most of it from Austria, or the boy
with the dog that keeps ringing his bell?
Will the landlord start believing me?
Should I put an ad in *Tagesspiegel*, saying
Heckewald is dead, *Heckewald ist tod?*

A Pig in God's Ear

Les morts sont des invisibles,
ils ne sont pas des absents –
so wrote St Augustine, according to
a wall of the Paris restaurant
Le Cochon à l'Oreille. A pig
in the ear, indeed, and Monsieur
le propriétaire is there himself
with his long grey hair and beard,
his yellow safety jacket, his cheering
of a fire engine that jangles past,
then his pointing to the drawing
of the stern woman above the quote –
his great grandma, *notre vierge noire*,
our Black Madonna. Also on the wall,
bright tile pictures of Les Halles market,
after the bell that announces
the end of selling, and the time
of the gleaners, or the arrival
by train at Rue Balthard, at 1 a.m.,
of the traders, or the stacked baskets
of raspberries and strawberries.
And ruling over all, a sculpture
in wood and iron, of a tall female
with chain locks, standing on a male
head, and across whom flies an angel
with saw wings and a dog's face.

That Meal

We shopped for that meal in three countries.
Not one of them had everything we wanted.
A passport was needed to fill our pantries.

A chef does time up in the gantries,
watching buildings that are glass-fronted.
We shopped for that meal in three countries.

Those who enjoyed it were from three countries –
in one of these our wild boar was hunted.
A passport was needed to fill our pantries.

Our goose-liver starter would beat all *entrées* –
served pink, with pears that were butter-anointed.
We shopped for that meal in three countries.

The wine we served came from rare vintries.
No wine-buff on earth would have been affronted.
A passport was needed to fill our pantries.

Everyone present was one of the sentries
of the short line, each of those indented.
We shopped for that meal in three countries.
A passport was needed to fill our pantries.

A Princess

My sister lay like a princess in her coffin,
not any princess, one who was special,
who now lay there, waiting to be woken.

The last words from her I'd heard spoken
were 'You smell of curry', said as if crucial.
My sister lay like a princess in her coffin.

She'd had a goodbye party that was a laugh-in
and that I'd missed. I was in Basel.
She now lay there, waiting to be woken.

I was away for most of her life in
a welter of countries, what a hassle!
My sister lay like a princess in her coffin.

I came back enough to see how tough in
her dying she was. In such hell.
Then she lay there, waiting to be woken.

She'd built her house in Ballyliffin,
where she was born. It was just as well.
My sister lay like a princess in her coffin.
She lay there, waiting to be woken.

Chop Suey

(after Edward Hopper)

They are sitting, not speaking,
across from each other
at a bare, white table. A squat
brown teapot points its spout
between them. One blue bowl
is empty, the other hidden.
There's no smile on the lipsticked
mouth we see, and the hands
are under the table. The other's
are on it, throwing shadows.
Behind them, a man is checking
his watch for a woman,
and behind him, two hills
cross on their way to the sky.
Where is the waiter to fill
their bowls, to bring fresh tea?
Chopsticks are out of the question,
certainly today. Has someone died?
They look like sisters in the dim
light through the painted window,
behind which, not yet lit up,
a large, bulb-studded 'E' waits
above the top of a 'Y'.

Doodle Doo

Doodle doo. And the light
drops thinly from the sun
on those up
                    and those not up –
such as me. And through the
half-open blinds I see
wisps of smoke wriggle
and flutter through the air,
then a magpie land on a wire,
and beyond this, a plane's
long, white, frizzy tail.
Oh year, are these your
final offerings – scraps
of aerial visuals? After all
the horses falling
                    at the final fence,
of course. After all the mud.
A crow hops from chimney pot
to chimney pot. A cloud
drifts above him.
                    Is that
a face at the skylight
in the grey slates? Whose?
Where is my sister?
The wire vibrates in the wind,
the sky spells rain,
the distant thunder of a plane
pulls me up. Ah, doodle doo.
                    Doodle doo.

Little Flower

Little flower, growing on the hillside,
facing the Atlantic. I don't know what you are.
I know you're wild, but I'm going to water you
from this bottle of Ballygowan. I want to tell you
a story of a small, small horse who decided
to gallop all the way to Antarctica, swimming
any sea that got in its way, ignoring people
who tried to jump on its back, surging past cameras,
past borders, past men who wanted to stop it,
all down the long, last leg of Argentina, through
Welsh- (not Irish-) speaking Tierra del Fuego,
till it plunged into the cold water and emerged
among the astounded penguins on that icy continent.
What do you think of that, little flower?
Would you like more water? Anything else?
If I didn't think you grew in the perfect place
I'd pluck you and wear you in my buttonhole,
then march into the local branch of Heaven.

Autumn

(after Trakl)

Under the beech trees whose brown leaves
are falling, the thorns are massing.
The wild purple flowers dance in the wind.
Seven flowerpots, empty except for weeds,
block the wilderness, beyond which cows
wade through yellow furze without mooing,
waiting for the rain that's always near.
A gull arrives, shrieking, from the sea,
alights on a lamppost and goes silent.
Black clouds congregate in the sky,
where a shiny grey helicopter hovers
before veering off above the hills
and out over the churning Atlantic
that tonight's crescent moon will float on.
The dead leaves twitch on the ground
behind the low wall that the thorn-stalks
poke over, encouraged by the rain
that now plummets down, as far off
in the village, the church bells start to ring,
making a dog howl till it goes hoarse.

The Deserter

He ran because he'd killed too many.
He hid in a barn outside the town
his sergeant had made him set ablaze,
and from the rafters he watched
the far-off dance of the flames. Asleep
he dreamed of a noose hanging, and
his head pushed through, although
when awake he knew it'd have to be
the spraying of a machine gun.
Some people had to be killed fast.

He thought back to his recruitment –
a one-legged veteran had thrown
his crutch into the air, and croaked
out *The Internationale*. A bugler played,
three girls did a dance, and a queue –
including him – lined up to sign up.
Had anyone done stupider than that?
A rat crept out to stare at him, then
quickly disappeared. He wanted it
to come back, to skitter all over him.

His Crows

Four crows flew in formation
above the train, and at Milton Keynes
they spread out into a wave
and veered towards Norfolk,
and the roof of that Old Church.

He was inside, dressed in black,
as always, meditating, and
drinking his dark red wine.
A glance at his black watch
sent him to the fridge, to take out

a long, marble plate, with four
dead mice on it, which he placed
on the altar he kept outside.
Each crow dived on a mouse,
till four skeletons lay on the plate.

He put on a CD of Nico's sepulchral
singing, and the crows sang along,
almost in tune, with him conducting.
Then he strode off to the back room
and his black, leather hammock.

Saxophone Man

Saxophone man, he come,
bright red hair, orange suit,
yellow hat with parrot feather,
smile as big as the sun.

He walk up Hauptstrasse,
stand at fountain and play.
The crows come to hear,
the children all run there.

Me, I'm slow, I limp after,
stand at back of throng,
listen to notes bend and
dance through a sad tune.

Then Redman, he walk,
he walk fast, still playing.
The children run after.
I try, but can't keep up.

Over the bridge he go,
over the bridge they tumble,
then down to the harbour,
to the very end of the pier.

I reach the first blue boat,
then the splashing start,
and ahead, I see them,
one by one, all jump in

and then, the music stop,
Saxophone man, he run
into woods at edge of town,
and he never seen again.

The Slow Story of No

Sing us a gypsy song,
set the accordion going
get the *tuica* flowing,
invite us to sing along,
making it up as we go,
but following you, as you tell
in a Carpathian howl
the slow story of no –

no Mercedes on the grass
next to the bottle bank,
no moustachioed men to thank
for clearing the rusty mess.
No, it happened organically,
like a mouse corpse rotting.
No heads were plotting.
The wheels rolled away.

The doors and windows walked,
the leather seats flew
over the morning dew.
No bystander gawked.
The engine gave a creak
and wrenched itself up
to float like a spaceship
into another week.

And the chassis that remained
let wind blow through it,
let children climb on it,
while old men complained,
and no thin, grey horse

chomped grass, until
his trailer was full –
with nothing, of course,

and no Mercedes on the grass,
the slow story of no.

Stone

I wasn't the highest stone
but I did make the crenel
of the northwest turret
where the flag flew – yellow
with three black boars on it.

I avoided the cannon balls,
unlike so many stones.
The rest of us became a ruin.
Children clambered up,
one fell down and died.

I tumbled down later
to be thrown in a pile
with other stones, covered
in green moss and birdshit,
and white, spindly weeds.

What I know is this –
we will all be reborn
in a stone house by a weir,
with two bay windows
and a huge granite arch.

I want the door red. I want
the darkest teak stairs inside.
I want my owner to be a prince
of rock music. I want to feel
guitar-chords bouncing off me.

The Piper's Cave

The young girls will be old women
when I return, when I return.
The young lambs will be old sheep
when I come back again.
So sang the redhaired piper,
as he vanished into the cave,
playing a frolicksome jig,
followed by a bouncy polka,
and he'd told his three friends
they'd track him by his music
seeping up through the black
earth and the green grass.
They danced and they sang,
they careered about, thinking
him the bravest piper that had
ever lived, here in the good
parish of Clonmany, or else-
where. And when a reel turned
them left, towards the sea,
they pranced that way, gladly,
and a gull flew low overhead,
joining in their singing, and a
crow almost cawed in tune,
until the music morphed into
a slow air, so sad the three
began weeping, then all went
silent. They were two miles
from where they'd started, just
in the townland of Annagh,
they shouted the piper's name –
no answer. They appealed to
the fairies – as much reponse

as from the trees. They trooped
back to the poteen, raising
glasses to their brave friend,
writing together a song to him.
The young lambs were old women
when he returned, returned.
The young girls were old sheep
when he came back again.

Fans

Seven horses climbed out of the Wannsee
and galloped, dripping, to Kleist's grave.
They neighed and bent their forelegs –
one rapped the stone gently with a hoof.
another came forward to lick the name.
Then, one by one, they felt a weight
drop on their backs, and a jab in the side
poke them into a joyful canter along
the big lake's bank. Such whinnying
had not been heard for centuries, thought
a man walking three barking terriers.
When each horse returned another left
till all seven had felt the rider's weight
then they stood in a ring around the grave
to neigh a soft, high-pitched chorus
before pulling off in strict formation
to trot in a row, heads high, back to where
they'd left the water, wade in again,
watched by a group of shrieking kids, then
swim in an arc towards the farther shore.

The Birds of Chamissoplatz

The birds sing at night in Chamissoplatz,
they sing of street-battles fought in 1945,
they sing of storms that will wreck their nests,
that will blow down their trees. They say: *Listen*
to the bird on the moon, the big white bird
who will fly down here when all is ruined –
the houses, the restaurants, the people –
when the air is too hot to breathe or fly in,
when the bicycles all have been melted,
the dog bones fused to the broken streets.

The birds sing this at night in Chamissoplatz,
say: *Drink water while you still have some,*
go for long walks in the bucketing rain,
visit the Antarctic while it's walkable on,
spend time in Holland while it still exists.
I hear them from the kitchen, the bathroom,
I hear them when I'm back in my bed,
and they keep me from falling asleep again.
I know they will be quiet in the morning –
only at night can they sing in Chamissoplatz.

Eternity Strand

I'm standing on Ballyliffin Strand,
the known end of the universe,
marvelling at the weird light
filtered through a pink cloud bank
that surely was created in hell
at the other end of eternity.

I get my head around eternity
when I come down to this strand
to look out over a sea that hell
can't accommodate in its universe –
that flings itself against a sandbank
to help create this curious light.

Painters arrive here for the light.
They've been coming for an eternity –
they deposit their work in the bank,
countless portraits of the strand,
sometimes portrayed as a hell
of all the yellows in the universe,

with all the blues of the universe
daubed there on top, and that light
radiating out for all eternity,
even seeping its way into hell.
Ah, how fortunate is the bank
to have these masterpieces of strand,

these visions of a perfect curved strand
that 'holds within it the universe'
(to quote the manager of the bank) –
that reflects and filters the sunlight,
sometimes suggesting a heat that hell
has aspired to for all eternity.

No, there's no other symbol of eternity
than this dazzling bow of a strand,
no other snapshot of hell
in any corner of the known universe,
disregarding all its sources of light –
and this is well-known at the bank.

They refer to it as *Eternity Strand*.
They say it shows hell in the universe.
They claim to be the Bank of Light.

Booty

Going down the hill
in a striped French teeshirt,
I met a thrush who
was bashing a snail
on the road, repeatedly,
while cars whizzed past,
then, as the road levelled,
and the river arrived,
I spied a heron, perched
on a half-submerged
supermarket trolley,
just before the sawn-off
stump of the vandalised
tree, newly peeled,
and sporting a sad face
in sketched black lines,
so I slunk on, to the
market, where I half-lived,
and I asked my butcher
for a cheap French cut.

The Yellow Golf Ball on the Lawn

Every time I come in the gate, I see it
lurking in the grass, beside the bio bin.
And I ask myself how it got here. We
are so far from any golf course, that no
golfer, however long-hitting, could loft
a ball that far. Could a dog have brought it?
I've never seen a dog invader, only
cats, and they wouldn't touch a golf ball.
Crows' beaks don't open wide enough,
nor even seagulls'. No, it has to be human –
but who? My neighbours are not golfers.
I know because I was one myself,
a long time ago, elsewhere, but still–
we walk in a certain way, hesitate
before making moves, take our bearings
from the sun, test the wind. Could it be
that I might have brought that ball here?

I lost many a golf ball when younger,
and once or twice they were yellow.
Not often, but I did try them sometimes.
And I remember the mysterious vanishing
of a yellow ball, when I was in danger
of winning a competition. We searched,
and searched, in vain. I had to add the
two penalty strokes, and lost, of course.
Could this be that ball – flown all the way
from Donegal to Cork, through four
decades, to lie there waiting for my shot?
But where is the flag and the green, and
more pertinently, where are my clubs?

What am I supposed to do – kick it?
Grab a gardening trowel and bury it?
Or should I pick the ball up tomorrow,
pocket it, and drop it in the River Lee?

Matthew Sweeney was born in Lifford, Co. Donegal, Ireland in 1952. He moved to London in 1973 and studied at the Polytechnic of North London and the University of Freiburg. After living in Berlin and Timişoara for several years, he returned to Ireland and now lives in Cork.

His poetry collections include: *A Dream of Maps* (1981), *A Round House* (1983) and *The Lame Waltzer* (1985) from Raven Arts Press; *Blue Shoes* (1989) and *Cacti* (1992) from Secker & Warburg; *The Bridal Suite* (1997), *A Smell of Fish* (2000), *Selected Poems* (2002), *Sanctuary* (2004) and *Black Moon* (2007) from Jonathan Cape; *The Night Post: A Selection* (Salt, 2010), and *Horse Music* (Bloodaxe Books, 2013), a Poetry Book Society Recommendation. *Black Moon* was shortlisted for the T.S. Eliot Prize and for the Irish Times Poetry Now Award. He has also published editions of selected poems in Canada (*Picnic on Ice*, Vehicule Press, 2002) and in Germany (*Rosa Milch*, bilingual tr. Jan Wagner, Berlin Verlag, 2008).

He won a Cholmondeley Award in 1987 and an Arts Council Writers' Award in 1999. He has also published poetry for children, with collections including *The Flying Spring Onion* (1992), *Fatso in the Red Suit* (1995) and *Up on the Roof: New and Selected Poems* (2001). His novels for children include *The Snow Vulture* (1992) and *Fox* (2002). He edited *The New Faber Book of Children's Poems* (2003) and *Walter De la Mare: Poems* (2006) for Faber; co-edited *Emergency Kit: Poems for Strange Times* (Faber, 1996) with Jo Shapcott; and co-wrote *Writing Poetry* (Teach Yourself series, Hodder, 1997) and the novel *Death Comes for the Poets* (Muswell Press, 2012) with John Hartley Williams.

Matthew Sweeney has held residencies at the University of East Anglia and the South Bank Centre in London, was Poet in Residence at the National Library for the Blind as part of the Poetry Places scheme run by the Poetry Society in London, and is currently writer-in-residence at University College Cork. He is a member of Aosdána.